My First Wild Animals
Copyright © 1989 by Bettina Paterson
First published in 1989 by William Heinemann, London, England,
under the title *Wild Animals*.

Library of Congress Cataloging-in-Publication Data
Paterson, Bettina.
  My first wild animals / Bettina Paterson.
    p.   cm.
  Summary: Labeled collage illustrations introduce such wild animals
as the orangutan, zebra, and kangaroo.
  ISBN 0-690-04771-1 : $. — ISBN 0-690-04773-8 (lib. bdg.) :
$
  1. Animals—Pictorial works—Juvenile literature. [1. Animals—
Pictorial works.] 2. Vocabulary. I. Title.
QL49.P3   1991   89-17305
599—dc20   CIP
                                                              AC

Printed in Hong Kong. All rights reserved.
        1 2 3 4 5 6 7 8 9 10
First American Edition, 1991

My First Wild Animals

Bettina Paterson

📖 HarperCollins*Publishers*

brown bear

orangutan

camel

alligator

polar bear

penguins

giraffe

rhinoceros

zebra

leopard

gorilla

buffalo

whale

koalas

elephant

walrus

hippopotamus

parrot

tiger

panda

kangaroos

seal

llama